HOW TO PREPARE YOUR
COMPANY OR BUSINESS IDEA
FOR OUTSIDE INVESTORS

PIXIE
DUST

FRANK DAPPAH

Co-Founder of Corvus
Web Services

DEDICATION

Dedicated to Bernice

TABLE OF CONTENTS

CHAPTER ONE

THE CHECKLIST

> "Give me six hours to chop down a tree and I will spend the first four sharpening the axe."
> — Abraham Lincoln

So, let's get the common sense, more technical stuff out of the way first. I am sure your interest in this book is a clear indication that you are either launching a new business and are looking for investors to help back your venture, or you have a business that is showing signs of growth, and you are looking for some ideas on how to approach investors to get the capital infusion you need to grow your company.

The kind of cash you need to buy supplies, spend on marketing, hire new employees, and so on. Well, you came to the right place! My reasons for writing this book really is to share some thoughts and ideas I may have on the subject.

I am basing these streams of consciousness, which I should caution may sometimes seem like the ravings of a weirdo, on my years of experience in business, and raising capital.

I am what you call an "**Opportunistic Entrepreneur**", Self-taught in every sense of the word. I only bring this up as a way to warn you that during the course of reading this book, you will find some of my ideas to be counterintuitive. Some of my views on certain aspects pertaining to the subject matter at hand will go against the prevailing conventional hypothesis out there. And that may be so, but keep in mind that l am only launching this literary projectile from a launchpad of experience and years of doing "it" myself.

These are methods and processes that have worked for me in the past, and some I still use today. With that being said, I would like us to go over the textbook steps you definitely should take before you think about approaching any kind of investor for your company.

The checklist before the checklist

Almost any expert you talk to, and by "Experts" I mean Lawyers, accountants, and any consultant you seek out to help you approach investors will require that you have checked off these items to put you in a position, both legally and structurally to take in outside capital.

We need a plan

A complete business plan is probably the most basic, yet important item to acquire. You cannot have a business without a clear plan.

A plan on where you want to go, and how you plan to get there. If nothing at all, you want your business plan to contain an overall summary of what your company stands for and how it makes or plans to make money.

For those of us who have zero ideas on where to start, I recommend you check out Liveplan (https://www.liveplan.com/) to get started on building a dynamic business plan.

Marketing plan

Most all-inclusive business plans will have a marketing plan. I, however, like to create a detailed plan whenever I decide to either invest in a startup, or start a new company. I actually think even more important than financial projections, you need to know exactly how you plan to get the word out about your products and/or services.

If you do not already have a **Sales and Marketing** machine in place, investors will want to hear how you plan to get your goods in the hands of your prospective customers.

Financial models

Just like with your business and marketing plans, any serious investor(s) will want to know what your financial models look like.

Do not underestimate the importance of this task. Try to get as detailed as possible. Include such elements as projected costs, acquisitions, sales, and revenue, including your profit margins, growth rates and when you expect the business to start making money. This will let investors know that you are looking to build a profitable business. One that can-someday-deliver a handsome return on investment.

Term sheet

A term sheet is a bullet-point document outlining the material terms and conditions of a business agreement. After a term sheet has been "executed", it guides legal counsel in the preparation of a proposed "final agreement".

If you are out and about looking for capital, and I mean seriously looking to bring on outside investors, you should have a term sheet. Let investors know exactly what the terms of their investment in your business will be.

Let folks know what you expect and what they can expect from you. If you are not just looking for money, but also looking for these guys to help you run your business, or perhaps introduce you to other investors, you should lay it all out in your term sheet.

Market overview/ research

Your market research, if you do not already have a market overview based on past business activities, is verifiable proof that there actually is a need for what you are selling or proposing.

You may be able to access market research through firms like Esri (www.esri.com), Experian(www.experian.com), or Consumer Reports (www.consumerreports.org) to put together detailed market research.

But of course, if you already have a thriving business, then you can create a market overview based on your sales, customer count, revenue, and profit figures.

CHAPTER TWO

TABLE FOR TWO?

"Great things in business are never done by one person. They're done by a team of people."
– Steve Jobs

Is your business meant to just feed you and your family, or is this something that can be much bigger?

Are you looking to have a small company?

You know, something nice and cute to call your own, or are you planning to, as they say, **"take it all the**

way to the top?".

This is but one of the many general factors to carefully examine before you put your business out there, looking for investors.

In this chapter, we shall walk through a few concepts to help prepare you for the idea of bringing other people into your business or partnering with some "money folks" to launch a new one.

Can you handle change?

I mean, can you? Because you know once you bring on outside investors, that's what is going to happen, right?

Everything will change. Not the fundamentals of the business of course, but more than likely, everything else about your business will undergo a metamorphosis.

You will all of a sudden have to be accountable to someone else. You will spend most of your days responding to emails, or taking in-person meetings with your investors, and even sometimes with their families and representatives.

You will have to take input from these folks- whose money you took - about everything having to do with your business. And you will do so because it will no longer be just **your business**. Be sure to prepare yourself, and your employees; and family members for change.

I once knew an entrepreneur who built a company with his Dad. The two men were not just partners, they also worked together on a day-to-day basis. At some point, they decided to bring on investors. He: the son, was able to deal with the change that come with the new capital. His father, on the other hand, was unable to handle the changes and ultimately left the company.

This entrepreneur in question soon followed in his Dad's footsteps because he did not want to work without his father.

The problem is, they did not truly appreciate and understand the changes that would occur as a result of bringing in outside investors. It will be in your best interest to truly prepare yourself to handle the inevitability of change.

It's a two-way street

Working with investors after their initial investment can be a challenging proposition.

Not unlike any other personal or professional relationship, you will get what you put into your dealings with your investors / partners. In these situations, something is always expected of you, and most folks fail to take that fact seriously.

Most people who are new to the Investor - entrepreneur relationship fail to understand the duality of such setups.

You often hear entrepreneurs express their frustration with the institutional investor class. Andy Dunn, co-founder of Bonobos Inc. Once said that 98% of all Venture Capitalists are dumb. This is of course a statistical impossibility, but one can see how unhappy he would have had to have been to say this publicly.

It takes two to tango, and the folks on the other end of the table will expect you and your team to show all the considerations, respect, communication, money can buy. In this case, their money. Failing to acknowledge and act accordingly Will cause disruptions to your business, which will hurt the operational integrity of your company.

For the sake of sanity, I suggest, in the strongest possible terms that the expectations on either side of the aisle are meticulously addressed before any long-term deals are struck.

Don't be a Yes man

Nobody likes a **YES** man. Well, or woman. In your dealings with your proposed investor partners, bankers, suppliers, and customers, it helps to avoid being agreeable just to avoid confrontational-ish situations.

Look, I am not saying that you shouldn't try to be as approachable and easy to work with as possible. Nope! I am definitely not recommending any perpetual existence of conflict between you and your financial backers. I am merely asking you not to prioritize smoothness of your work relationships over taking the necessary actions to do what is best for your business.

Remember, this is your vision. You built this business. You are the guardian of the future of this firm. Sure, you want to be open to new ideas and new ways to look at things. You most definitely want you to speak up when you are certain some actions will produce adverse outcomes. Don't just go along to get along. You won't be doing yourself and your employees any favors.

Letting go of your baby
Most entrepreneurs feel a certain level of emotional connection with the businesses they start, run, or even conceive of. If you are the enterprising, self-starter type, you know what I am talking about.

Being an entrepreneur, for many of us is an absolute quality. It's the only Moniker of significance. It's not what we do, it's who we are, and separating us from that way of life would leave many of us without a purpose. We are passionate about our ideas and the businesses that emerge out of them.

We are connected to our customers, partners, employees, and every aspect of the organization's we run. Sometimes, allowing your company to receive outside capital can lead to you not being involved in the day-to-day running of the business anymore.

We are sometimes required, as a condition of an investment deal to step aside and let someone else run the firm.

This, and other similar circumstances can lead to you ultimately being on the outside looking in. You need to carefully consider this as a possible outcome, and work to emotionally, and psychologically reconcile this distinct possibility before going to find folks to invest in your company.

They don't have to "get it"

Going back to this notion that investors are dumb, or ruthless, or my personal favorite- Just don't get it. I feel as though, as valid as some of these sentiments may seem from the entrepreneur's standpoint, it is important to realize that asking, or expecting your investors to see things your way, or even have the same level of cohesion with your company past the reasons for which they invested is a big ask.

I have this opinion because I think looking at things this way ignores a blatant reality - **they don't have to get it!**

I mean, think about it. Your Grocer doesn't expect you to understand and empathize with the difficulty and logistical bête noire it is to get those apples, spinach and stuff to the store. And why not? Because you don't care. All you want is to be able to walk in and buy your stuff and move on with the rest of your day. How the stuff gets there? Not your problem.

If you are wondering which one of these folks you are in this scenario? Well, you my friend are the Grocer, oh and the groceries? Cash! Yes, that's right, money, greenbacks, el guapo. Whatever you call it. That is why these guys and gals in suits are talking to you in the first place. They want to make money, and they see your company as being able to potentially deliver on that idea.

They could care less about where you got the inspiration, or how this was all a dream to one day save the world, one inexpensive pair of shoes a time. That story, I swear to you only matters to you. Ever notice how, on ABC's Shark Tank, the Sharks never really seem that interested in a business till the entrepreneur spits out how much money the company is making?

Keep this in mind. It's not that they don't get the business' back story, it's that they don't have to, and usually, don't care.

They just need to know if there is a potential to get a return on their investment. The only part of the pitch that carries weight initially is the **"money"** part.

CHAPTER THREE

THE COMPANY YOU KEEP

"Success? I don't know what that word means. I'm happy. But success, that goes back to what in somebody's eyes success means. For me, success is inner peace. That's a good day for me."
-- Denzel Washington

Making the decision to bring on an Angel investor, VC, or any other kind of investor is one that should not be taken lightly.

This is arguably one of the most important decisions you'll ever make as far as your business is concerned.

Not unlike a marriage, the type of investor(s) you partner with will greatly influence your trajectory as an organization, and sometimes on a personal level as well.

Remember, these are folks with who you will spend countless hours. Your level of comfort is very important. You will want to be in business with folks you, at the very least like being around.

Most entrepreneurs view investors as just sources of money, just a guy or gal who writes the checks. I often encounter folks who seem to believe that an investor is one who simply provides the cash needed to grow or launch a business idea, and then stays out of the way.

I actually make it a point not to invest in any business unless the founders are open to hearing what I have to say about their business model, industry, and so on.

I am typically not looking for them – the founders - to take and / or adopt any of my ideas, nope! I just want to make sure that these are folks who are open to new ideas, and if need be, will be open to my, or the input of any other professionals.

In this chapter, I will talk to you a bit about the things you will want to look for in any potential investor.
You will want to be frank with yourself and the

folks you ask to invest in your business about what you expect, and what they can expect from you.

Are you looking for an investment of time and money?

Be clear with yourself about this particular point even before you go out to solicit investment capital. Also be sure to communicate with any potential investor as precisely as possible about what you expect in this context.

Ask them if they are able to also avail themselves from - time to time to serve as a consultant to you and your team. Most institutional investors have spent years in "the field" gaining operational and strategic experience in many industries.

The average investor would have also devoted a considerable amount of time cultivating valuable relationships with bankers, lawyers, and other entrepreneurs. Be sure to position yourself to be able to tap into these resources as often as possible. And an investor's willingness, or lack thereof, to facilitate your exposure to their contacts and wisdom should be a prerequisite to be able to invest in your company.

The good news is, most investors will be more than happy to introduce you to as many people and organizations as it takes to help you succeed.

Expectation of expertise

Beyond money, what does, or will your company need that you believe Someone, or folks in the investor class can provide?

As I have said before, a percentage of Angel investors and Venture capitalists invest in areas in which they possess years of experience and expertise. According to a recent survey by Tech news giant, TechCrunch, general partners at top-tier VC firms often have experience as founders or senior executives at entrepreneurial companies.

On average, 40 percent of the current partners at high-performing investment houses are experienced entrepreneurs, and almost one-fifth of them are former C-level executives at startups.

You and your company can be the beneficiaries of this indispensable cache of resources. Ones that transcends money.

I would advise that you carefully assess the existence of these post-Series A needs and decide as to which mix of expertise and / or experience, along with cash that you will need going forward.

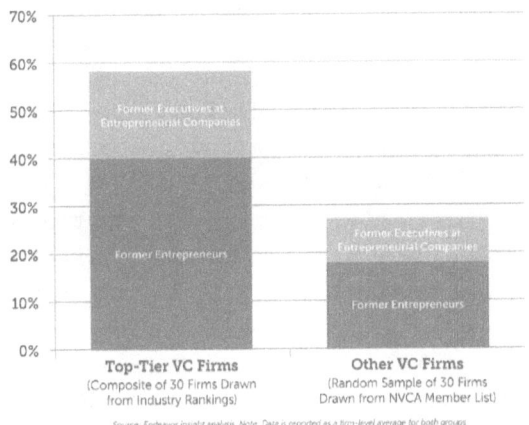

Entrepreneurial Experience Among Active General Partners

Top-Tier VC Firms
(Composite of 30 Firms Drawn
from Industry Rankings)

Other VC Firms
(Random Sample of 30 Firms
Drawn from NVCA Member List)

Source: Endeavor Insight analysis. Note: Data is reported as a firm-level average for both groups.

Time horizon

It takes time for most businesses to get started, flourish, and reach its full potential. There are no overnight successes in business, despite what the media tries to tell us.

Facebook was a 10-15-year overnight success story. The average time between a deal and exit by a VC is between 8 - 10 years.

The idea that starting a new company, that is if you intend to grow it into any respectably sized firm, takes time, should be one that you are used to.

This message should be delivered precisely and clearly to any new partners you decide to bring into the fold. They- your new partner, should expect to be committed (long-term) to helping grow the business.

Yes, most, if not all investors go into partnerships with Startups with the clear goal of some kind of future exit. Often times, this ambition on the Investor's part will be clearly stated in any term sheet presented.

That is the nature of any deal. Unless you come to some sort of alternative funding arrangement, any VC or Angel investor will, at some point want to cash-out of the deal.

What you need to be on the same page with any potential investor about, however, is how long either of you expects it to take to be able to realize said exit.

This is one of those critical issues you will not want to assume or shy away from before, during, and after any deal is struck.

Portfolio companies

Aside from individual investors, Angels, friends, and family. Most institutional investors go out and raise funds for the purpose of investing in other companies.

The way it works is that these professionals - Venture capitalists, private equity guys, and gals solicit cash from high net worth individuals, financial institutions, and other funds. They then pour this new cash haul into specific startups. The "Money Guys" get a fee (from investors of their funds) for their expertise and a percentage of any profits realized as a result of an exit.

Most Investors select certain industries and markets to invest in. It is not uncommon for a single investor to have their hands in multiple companies in the same space, at the same time.

There are various schools of thought out there as to whether these kinds of situations benefit the Startups being funded, or do these arrangements merely serve as a way for institutional investors to hedge their bets in any particular industry.

Some believe that entrepreneurs can benefit from the shared wisdom and familiarity with any potential issues anticipated as a result of these types of situations.

Others don't seem to think any one company stands to gain if their VC partners simply see them as a financial instrument; just one of many eggs in the basket.

Either way, this is a question you want to ask any potential investor before you finalize any arrangements. If the answer is "Yes, we do have other companies like yours in our portfolio", I suggest taking the time to meet with the other founders and see if this works for you. Also ask the Investor to explain to you the strategy behind backing various competing entities, and how this benefits you and your firm.

Followup funds

No long-term investment takes a single lump sum of cash. I know this is how most people think it works: You go into a meeting with potential investors, you say you need $1 million to go from point A to B, the Angel investor or VC writes the check and that's it. You go out there and everything happens exactly like you thought it would.

The truth is, it is almost a statistical impossibility that stuff go according to plan, ever.

Most startups, beyond the Seed capital stage, will require four startup funding rounds: Seed, Series A, Series B, and Series C.

During your negotiations with your potential investor(s), you will either underestimate the amount of cash you really need, or how much it will take to build your business. You will more than likely need to raise more funds at some point.

This is a reality most folks with experience are all too familiar with. You need to know if your new investor is open to providing additional funding in the future should you need it, and what their terms will be.

Will they be willing to invest at the company's book value at that time, or will they look for any special considerations?

You want to, along with any consultants you bring on, have this conversation with any potential investors before you commit to any deal.

AGE TO IPO

The Next Billion Dollar Startups List

Average Years to IPO   Average No. Rounds of Financing to IPO

Source: VentureSource 12/31/2014

CHAPTER FOUR

DO YOUR HOMEWORK

"By failing to prepare, you are preparing to fail."
— Benjamin Franklin

They say success is mostly "**showing up**". This is true in most cases, especially in business. I would add that we give ourselves a much better chance at success when we show up prepared and armed with the knowledge and insights required to navigate any conundrums that befall us.

At this point, we want to address the need to try to conduct a thorough background search on any investors you are considering approaching.

So far, we have discussed some of the more internal monologue-ish concerns. With this particular chapter, however, we want to address the issue of **Due diligence**.

Perhaps more specifically, the idea of conducting your own version of due diligence on your target investors.

Below, I present a few pointers to consider while perusing insights on your new investor's background.

Other investors and entrepreneurs

An understandably logical genesis point - getting Facetime with those who have dealt with said investor in a similar capacity can help set the tone for your next step, or even help assess whether any further discussions are even necessary.

I would like to add that this kind of "digging" into the backgrounds of investors does not have to happen in secret. Let folks know you are talking to other folks about their past dealings. Not only will you get an idea of what to expect from said investor, but you will be getting a take on their track records from those who share your perspective and unique needs.

I mean, if you ask a banker what they think of a VC that is "winning" and making loads of money for the bank, the banker will say they are awesome - they produce results. This is because "success" to the bank may differ from the perspective of say, an employee of the same investor.

An entrepreneur with whom the firm or Angel has previously dealt with might not share that sentiment. You want to seek the feedback of folks who have been in your position before, as it relates to your prospective investor.

Financials

In business, nothing tells a story quite like the numbers. A company's financial reporting is the holy grail of analytical data. You will be able to quickly ascertain any potential issues an organization may have by reviewing its financials.

Now, I understand that " the numbers" might be more difficult to obtain when looking at individual investors and other non-institutional backers. There are, however, other comparable records you could obtain. You can go over the details of a potential investor's past deals, obtain bank statements, accounting records, tax returns, and other types of personal financial documents.

The idea is to get your hands on any document(s) from which you can get an idea of the financial health of your future backer(s).

Most serious investors will be more than happy to provide you with any information you require to help ease any concerns you may have about any impending deals.

Failing to do so (on the investor's part) might be a red flag.

Past deals

Other than reviewing the financial inner workings of a VC or Angel investor, one's past deals can help you understand the strategic strengths and weaknesses of an investing entity or individual.

You will be able to put a finer point on some of the concepts discussed in this book.

An investor's past deals will help you, among others, determine:

Area or industry of concentration - Understanding the area of concentration as it relates to your proposed investors' portfolio(s) will provide some clarity on various topics such as how invested they are in any particular industry, or their view on the direction on any space.

You will also know if they are spread a little thin by the size of their portfolio startups.

Average deal and typical exit point or time - We talked a little bit about this in a previous chapter. Looking at a table of past investments will also help you gauge your proposed investor's time horizon.

Typical number of rounds - Since you know by now that you will probably need to do a few more fundraising rounds, it helps to only, or mostly seek out investors who will typically continue to provide funding to their portfolio companies. That is, if the startup in question still operates in a way that still fits the investment strategy of the investor.

Basic research

As an entrepreneur living in the digital age, you are blessed to have literally terabytes of data at your fingertips at all times.

You can have access to tons of data about any professional investor with just the click of a mouse.

You can do some basic research online to gather a whole lot of information about your investor-partners.

You can access their websites, social media accounts, blog posts, and so on to learn a whole lot about them.

On the other hand, the lack of availability of information on such a basic level could also spell trouble, unless you are talking to a private investor.

Any respectable Angel or VC will have some kind of information about their firm online.

CHAPTER FIVE

HEALTH CHECK

"The road to success and the road to failure are almost exactly the same."
-- Colin R. Davis

One of the things I have come to realize as I approach my 40's is how important it is to be prepared. I know I have talked about this a bit in this book already but allow me to elaborate a bit.

There are various levels to preparation, I think. I also believe that most of us focus on the cosmetic aspects of being prepared. We like to dress things up to make them Look Good.

There is a very similar dynamic when it comes to marriage or forming long term life partnerships.

There are those who seek to make structural modifications to their personalities, attitudes, etc. To make us more conducive to living our lives with others, and those who only look to appear to be great partners at the outset of their relationships.

The latter always causes issues down the line. The same can be said for any entrepreneur-Investor relationship.

It is not enough to make your company look super investable. It is super important to fix any fundamental issues that may exist within your firm before looking for outside capital.

I assure you that any real issues that you try to mask will, at the least opportune time rear its ugly head, leading your investors (in some cases) to think your omission was deliberate. And you do not want those kinds of problems.

In this chapter, we shall address some of the most common things entrepreneurs should look to fix before taking on outside investors.

Churn

Churn may not be applicable to your business. This is more of an issue for businesses that rely on some kind of recurring payments from their customers.

Churn rate, in its broadest sense, is a measure of the number of individuals or items moving out of a collective group over a specific period.

Specifically, however, Churn will be the rate at which your subscribers cancel their subscriptions or stop paying their monthly, or annual subscription fees.

Although some level of churn is to be expected, you should keep a close eye on your churn rate as it compares to the rate at which new customers are subscribing to your service.

A typical "good" churn rate for SaaS companies that target small businesses is 3-5% monthly. The larger the businesses you target, the lower your churn rate has to be as the market is smaller.

For an enterprise-level product (talking $100,000-$1,000,000 per month), churn should be < 1% monthly. Most Startups, especially in the Software space will, in the first 1 - 5 years have a churn rate of over 10%. This is due to most firms still trying to figure out what their product actually does, and who it does it for. Most new Saas products will also have some bugs in the early years, causing a higher churn rate.

An unusually high churn rate could be signs of some serious fundamental problems in your business. The most common causes of higher than usual churn rates are **ineffective marketing**, **Product functionality**, and **product compatibility**.

I would strongly recommend that you take a look at your churn rate and compare it to your industry peers to get an understanding of where you are. If you find out that you have an unusually high churn rate, you could start to try to fix this issue by communicating with your past and current customers to get an overview of where things went wrong.

You could send out surveys to your customer list using tools like Survey Monkey (https://www.surveymonkey.com/) to see where to start. Here, feedback from your current and past customers is supremely important if you are to try to fix any issues with your product. You will have to see things from the point of view of your users. I know you believe you have a superior product. I get it. Your users/ customers, on the other hand may not feel this way. And when it comes to user experience, the only opinion that matters is the opinion of the user(s).

Sales

Sales to me is one of the most important aspects of your business, If not the most important. Entrepreneurs, I believe should focus on their company's sales team and sales strategy right from the beginning.

According to the U.S Small Business Administration, the number one reason for small business startup failure is due to a **lack of market need**. That is correct, 42 percent of all new businesses fail within the first 5 years due to their inability to get their target audience to exchange money for their products.

Having a strong sales system in place will prove to your investors that there is indeed a need for your product or service.

You should have two things on your mind when you start a business: Product development and Sales/Marketing.

This is just how I feel. I don't think one can truly build a profitable business without making Sales a priority.

This is where it all begins. Even if you are not quite profitable yet, most investors will want to see that you and your team can put points on the board, so to speak. Investors will want to know that you, at least have developed a robust system through which you are able to get your product in the hands of new customers on a consistent basis.

Investors will also want to know if you can create a sales and marketing system that costs the company less than the revenue gained by selling your products and/or services.

Improving sales, or building a sales apparatus is great for you as well in terms of the process of getting investor funds. This is because once you have the cash, you will know exactly how to deploy your newly found cash haul in ways that will produce a healthy return on investment for you and your partners.

Profitability (if you can help it)

The whole point of building a business is to make a profit at the end of the day. We want to be able to take home some cash after the revenue from the sale of our products and/or services results in excess money after we pay our cost of production, overhead, and taxes.

That being said, I am uniquely aware of how much of an elusive beast that goal can be. Some companies go for years without actually making a profit. Sure, they sell their stuff, and have paying customers, but somewhere along the way, they are unable to net any money after all bills are paid.

If you are in this position, fear not. This is a common phenomenon. **Twitter**, **Snapchat** and **Uber** are prime examples of firms that have hundreds of millions of users and customers but barely make any real money. These firms typically have plans to make a profit in the future and simply use investor funds to power the journey until then.

So, I want you to understand that you can go out and get investors without making a profit. I just think, for so many reasons that if you can execute on a profit-generating plan prior to asking investors to join you, you should. You should definitely do that! For one, this will help validate your company in a more vivid way. Nothing says *"We have a sustainable business model"* quite like profitability.

A Clear Exit Strategy

Whether you have a clear exit strategy in place or not will be important if you plan to exchange equity in your company for capital from investors.

Most Angel Investors and Venture Capital firms will want stock in your business. The Friends and Family crowd will typically come to some kind of payment terms with you when they help provide funding for your new business.

With your loved ones, you simply have to be able to pay them back what you owe them and be on your merry way.

CHAPTER SIX

EXIT STAGE LEFT

"Change is inevitable—except from a vending machine."
—Robert C Gallagher

In this chapter, I would like us to unpack the idea of an "exit strategy" a bit.

I think this is important for many reasons. I often run into quite a few entrepreneurs who have either built a solid business, and are looking for the added capital needed to, as they say, " *take their businesses to the next level*", or ones that are seeking investment capital to start a new business.

Typically, the entrepreneur, as passionate and competent as they may be, often never gives any thoughts to how they plan to return capital + growth back to their investors, employees and partners.

For some, this is merely an oversight, and for others, there are some emotional attachment issues around the topic. Some don't see the day when they let go of total control of their companies as a day that should even be considered.

Let's be honest, "exiting" a business is a topic of discussion primarily among business school folks, Bankers, and professional investors.

Assuming you are not a member of these groups of folks, I would like to address the most common exit options and ways to think about and approach the topic as a whole.

Defining your exit
You should always look for an exit plan that you are comfortable with.
One that not only meets the needs of you and your investors, but also the needs of your employees, vendors, and all others who will be affected by any such transition.

We want to be sure that we consider an option that is suitable for your type of business and is realistic, giving your time horizon and growth rate. You want to plan and execute an exit that will ensure that you have as much upside as possible relevant to whatever role you will look to play in the company, or not, post-exit.

Mark Zuckerberg, for example orchestrated an IPO that, although gave ownership to his shareholders, still allowed him to maintain control over the day-to-day operations at Facebook. As angry as Investors, shareholders, and the general public were during the whole post-2016 elections / Cambridge Analytica scandal, you will notice that Mark still maintained control of the social media giant he helped build. This is due to his iron grip on the board. The idea of relieving him of his duties never even came up in any serious way. This is due to his almost complete control over the management and governance of Facebook.

You will want to clearly consider which exit strategies will work for your business and be sure to clearly communicate this with any potential investors.

Carve out some time during your negotiations to fully address this topic, going into great detail to assure investors that this is something you have spent some time thinking about.

All on the same page
Communication is key in any meaningful interaction or relationship in life. Such is the same in business. It is always a good idea to communicate concisely and honestly with your employees, partners and investors.

The Exit Strategy question is one that should be addressed in a way that leaves very little room for misinterpretation or ambiguity. The fact is, most VC's and Angels simply want a meaningful return on the capital they deploy. Most investment houses look at opportunities that have the potential to produce at the very least, a 10x return.

This is just the nature of the business. They are in it to make money, and nothing else.

That being said, they also know that some type of large exit is required for this goal to be accomplished. Sure, equity investors typically have longer time horizons than other traditional lenders, but ultimately all parties who choose to invest in your business are looking for some kind of payday.

So, you may want to *build a world-class company that is growing and increasingly profitable over time*. That's what you want, but the only reason these folks will do business with you is if they can cash out at some point.

Let me note though, that there are some arrangements that will be mostly based on some agreement of ongoing profit sharing, but those are rare and mostly non-existent on a large scale.

MOST COMMON TYPES OF EXITS

Initial Public Offering (IPO): The IPO, which is the exit of choice for most highflying, well known startups is the first time a company sells stock to the general public.

Up until that point, a company's shareholders will consist mostly of its founders, employees, and other institutional investors. The main reason companies "*Go public*" is to provide a way for the firm's original investors to cash out, wholly or partially and also provide much needed capital for growth.

Depending on which country your business is located in, or on which nation's stock market you want to list your shares, pulling off an IPO can be a significantly laborious task. One that requires hours of preparation and complex reporting, not to mention the regulatory hurdles involved.

You should also note that the success of a public offering can be heavily dependent on the market's appetite for a company like yours, and/or the general economic climate at the time of your offering.

Companies like Facebook, although very successful now, struggled at the outset of their Initial public offering to gain traction. The stock price lagged its peers for months.

The market just couldn't quite understand Facebook's business model.

IPO's, one should note are also very rare - only 100-200 per year – compared to the number of startups launched per year.

Number of IPOs in the United States from 1999 to 2018

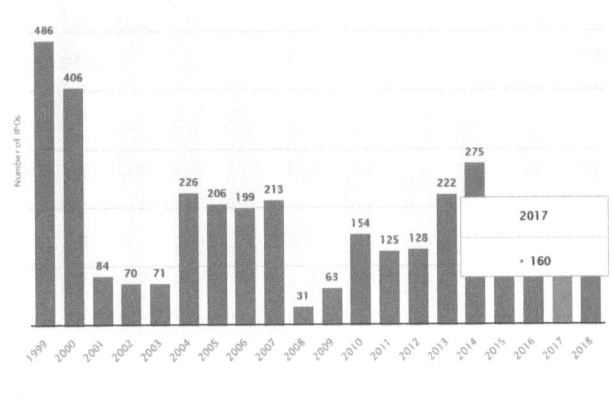

Number of IPOs

| 1999 | 2000 | 2001 | 2002 | 2003 | 2004 | 2005 | 2006 | 2007 | 2008 | 2009 | 2010 | 2011 | 2012 | 2013 | 2014 | 2015 | 2016 | 2017 | 2018 |

486, 406, 84, 70, 71, 226, 206, 199, 213, 31, 63, 154, 125, 128, 222, 275

2017

· 160

© Statista 2019

Regulation A+: Regulation A+ is a slimmed-down version of an IPO. This route allows you to list your company on an Exchange once you qualify. Using Regulation, A+ allows you to take the steps required to be compliant with the laws set out by the Securities and Exchange Commission (SEC) without having to publish accounts publicly or file other mandatory paperwork that would be required of an IPO.

Ben & Jerry's ice cream is best known for using this strategy to raise money from the public. Since the passage of the Jumpstart Our Business Startups or JOBS Act in 2012, and the subsequent rulings by the SEC making it legal to raise money from large groups of people on the internet, this regulation will catapult nationally 2016 as it quietly passed into law July 19, 2015.

Previously, under Regulation A, companies could not raise more than $20 million, but the Obama administration revised the law (which is now called Regulation A+) allowing entrepreneurs such as yourself to raise up to $50 million from the general public.

One of the great things about using Regulation A+ to raise money is that you do not need to hire any pricey lawyers or consultants to assist.

You can use this method to test the markets to see if there is an appetite for companies like yours before committing the $50,000+ required under this law.

Title III Crowdfunding: Another feature of the **JOBS Act** is Title III. This provision allows startup firms to raise money from the public using Crowdfunding.

According to the SEC, "Crowdfunding" generally refers to the use of the Internet by small businesses to raise capital through limited investments from a large number of investors.

Under SEC rules, the general public can invest in capital raising by start-up companies.

What Are the Rules?
Title III of the JOBS Act established crowdfunding provisions that allow early-stage businesses to offer and sell securities. The SEC subsequently adopted

Regulation Crowdfunding to implement the crowdfunding provisions of the JOBS Act. The role of the Financial Industry Regulatory Authority (FINRA) is to oversee the registration of crowdfunding portals and to ensure that they comply with the federal securities laws and FINRA rules.

Broker-dealers and funding portals that are registered with the SEC and are FINRA members are permitted to offer and sell securities on behalf of issuers to the investing public using crowdfunding.

Who Can Invest?

Like stocks and bonds, anyone can invest in crowdfunding offerings. But because of the risks involved, you are limited in how much you can invest during any 12-month period in these kinds of securities. The inflation-adjusted investment limits depend on your net worth and annual income:

- If either your annual income or your net worth is less than $107,000, then during any 12-month period, you can invest up to the greater of either $2,200 or five percent of the lesser of your annual income or net worth.

- If both your annual income and your net worth are equal to or more than $107,000 then, during any 12-month period, you can invest up to 10 percent of your annual income or net worth, whichever is less, but not to exceed $107,000.

Say your annual income is $150,000 and your net worth is $80,000. JOBS Act crowdfunding rules allow you to invest the greater of $2,200 or five percent of $80,000 ($4,000) during a 12-month period. So, in this case, you can invest $4,000 over a 12-month period.

Is this right for me?

Crowdfunding under Title III of the JOBS Act can be a great way to easily and quickly raise capital to grow your startup. The idea is to follow a process that will help you build up your cash reserves to grow your business and, in some cases, return capital to your initial investors.

As an entrepreneur, you want to take the time to familiarize yourself with all the rules and regulations associated with using Title III. You can visit the FINRA (www.finra.org) to learn as much as you can. You will also want to think about which crowdfunding portal works best for you.

Below, I have listed a few that you might want to take a look at as you consider raising cash this way.

StartEngine

www.startengine.com

Founded in 2014, StartEngine is the largest equity

crowdfunding platform in the US. According to the firm, their mission is to help entrepreneurs achieve their dreams by democratizing access to capital. They have launched more Reg CF offerings than any other platform and have successfully funded 275+ companies.

Highlights

- $4.6M+ in revenue for 2018, demonstrating year over year growth of 129%
- $100M+ raised on our platform
- 200,000+ registered users
- 22% of investors participate in more than one offering
- The average investment amount on StartEngine is $1,300

AngelList

www.angel.co

Founded in 2010, AngelList is one of the oldest and most established equity crowdfunding platforms. It was originally conceived to broker connections between cash-strapped technology entrepreneurs and angel investors – high-net-worth, tech-savvy funders, many of whom earned their fortunes by selling out of their own successful startups.

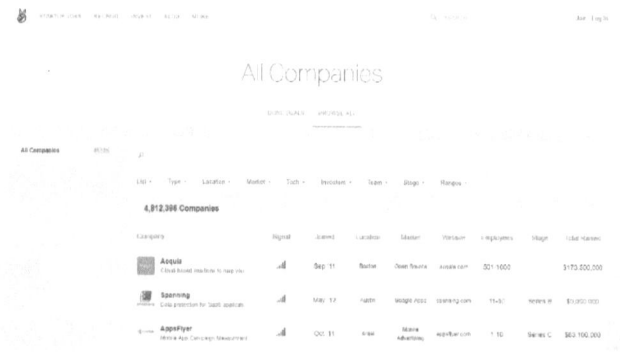

CircleUp

CircleUp connects investors with consumer-facing startups, mostly in the technology, fitness, and food and beverage sectors. Most companies have at least $1 million in revenue, and all "have a tangible product or retail outlet that you can touch, taste, use, or visit." CircleUp's machine learning engine, Helio, evaluates more than 1 million companies on billions of individual data points to pick the most promising startups from the pack.

www.circleup.com

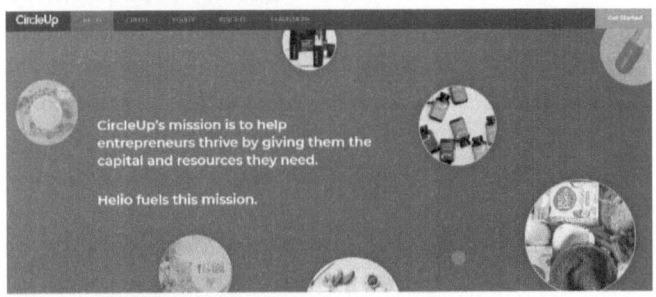

Highlights

Flexible Capital Solutions: They provide capital in the form of equity, credit, or both, based on your business's unique needs

Exclusive Data-driven Insights: Proprietary consumer market insights through Helio, their machine learning platform, gives you a knowledge advantage

An Unparalleled Network: Their vast network of entrepreneurs, institutional investors, retailers and industry experts gets you the resources you need.

Merger/ (Acquisition): A merger or acquisition can be a great way to return capital to your initial investors. This option unites two companies with shared strategic interests.

Typically, in your case, a merger will help you if and when you get a larger, deep-pocketed competitor to buy your company.

If you choose this as a means to provide an exit for your investors, you might want to build your firm with this in mind. In other words, you will want to look to build your company based on some strategic advantages that larger competitors might benefit from but have ignored or overlooked.

For example, if you are building a financial services firm, and look to one day sell your company to a larger bank or insurance company, then you might want to make technology and efficiency the cornerstone of your company.

This way, you will be able to sell your company to a larger, more traditional firm. One that will stand to benefit from your more updated way of conducting business.

CHAPTER SEVEN

PITCH PERFECT

"All progress takes place outside the comfort zone."
-- Michael John Bobak

Are you the founder of a rapidly growing startup? Have you reached the part in your growth story where bootstrapping just won't cut it anymore? Are you ready to build a robust sales team to go out and sell the heck out of your new product?

If you answered "Yes" to any two of these three questions, then you might be ready to receive outside capital.

You might want to start looking for your first Angel investor or Venture Capital partner. Remember: angel investors get approached every day about startups looking for funding. they turn down about 90 percent of the companies that pitch them.

What can you do to increase your chances of getting funded?

Have a well-thought-out presentation. Your presentation is your first, and sometimes last chance to make an impression on any potential investor. You should take some time out of your busy routines to perfect your pitch.

In this chapter, I will walk you through various aspects and components of the perfect investor pitch. I will also identify certain aspects of your story you want to present to prospective investors.

The Elevator pitch

The elevator pitch is a brief but pointed speech meant to spark interest and educate any potential investor on what your company does and the upside to investing in your firm. An effective elevator pitch should last no longer than 20 to 30 seconds.

Creating an elevator pitch

Constantly working and reworking your elevator pitch is the only way to make sure that you have the "best" version of your pitch at any given time. You will most likely go through various versions of your pitch in order to get one that you are pleased with.

Identify Your Goal

As an entrepreneur, you will want to start thinking about your elevator pitch in a way that puts your ultimate goal front and center. The idea is to start with a basic understanding of what you want your pitch if nothing else to communicate.

Since you will be talking to prospective investors, you will want to clearly demonstrate the value and potential for a return on their investment.

What do you do?

One of the most common and effective ways to start your pitch is with what your company does. It helps to speak as clearly and unambiguously as possible. Focus on the problems that you solve and how you help people. If you can, add information or a statistic that shows the value in what you do.

Your pitch, should, first of all, excite your audience, leading them to want to hear more. Be as clear and simple as possible when describing what it is your firm does. There really is no need for fancy language here. Speak in terms that even a 5-year old could understand. If not, you will leave your audience going "Oh, that's great", at which point you will see most of them simply go quiet. And in sales, **no questions** is a bad sign.

Example:

" We build software applications and mobile apps to help large businesses train their new employees."

State your Unique Selling Position (USP)

Your Unique Selling Position should be clearly communicated in your elevator pitch. You will want to let investors know exactly what makes you, your organization, or your idea, unique. Be sure to follow up your " What you do" statement with your USP.

Example:

"We employ a direct approach. We are able to retain more clients than our competitors by assigning each client with their own account executive to help address their unique needs"

Engage with a Question

Be sure to follow up your statement of USP with open-ended questions (questions that can't be answered with a "yes" or "no" answer). This is a great way to get your audience to engage with you in a meaningful way.

Example

" What is your company's investment plan this year? What spaces or industries are you guys looking at for this year?"

Your Pitch Deck
This is a brief, concise presentation used to provide your prospective investors with a quick overview of your business plan. A pitch deck is often built using PowerPoint, Keynote or Prezi, and is mostly used as an illustrative tool during in-person or online meetings with potential investors, customers, partners, and co-founders.

This is how we do it

I often run into entrepreneurs like yourself looking for funding who struggle with the task of creating an effective pitch deck. In an attempt to help you navigate this often-daunting task, I have created a step-by-step guide (*via inc.com*) to help you create an effective pitch deck.

Slide 1: Statement of purpose.

When I talk with a young entrepreneur, I always start by asking, "What's the big idea?" What I'm looking for is a statement about who they are and what they do in a sentence so elemental and polished as to adorn a statue.

This isn't just the elevator pitch; this is the pitch you need to get out before the elevator doors have closed in the lobby.

This statement is worth spending a remarkable amount of time on, because it might be the most valuable dozen words you'll ever assemble.

It's something that needs to be torn up and debated and rewritten a thousand times. It also needs to be a living statement that can grow and change as you learn about your business, what happens in your marketplace, what matters to investors, the zeitgeist, and the thousand other factors that will be crucial to the growth of your business.

And if your first slide is lacking it, your deck is like a book with a bad cover--nobody's going to buy it.

Slide 2: Show off your team.

Ever go to the oh-so-fancy movie theater where the usher (kind of uncomfortably, in my opinion) comes out in front of everyone to tell you what the movie is about? That's exactly what you did in the first slide.

In Slide 2, the lights go down, the movie starts, and your audience gets to see how this whole thing is going to unfold--beginning with meeting your main characters. And what are investors looking for in your team? Three things, really: that they've done it before, that they're the best at what they do, and that they're incredibly charismatic.

Think charisma isn't a gigantic factor in a funding decision? Then you're forgetting that dogs would be mere members of the wild kingdom if not for being gifted with oodles of the stuff.

So, bring as much of your team as you think helps your cause and show off the veritable tour de force of talent that's going to give the room absolute confidence you can pull off everything you're about to lay out.

Slide 3: Identify the problem.

If you're pursuing the kind of big idea that matters to venture capitalists, you need to comprehensively and clearly identify the fundamental problem you're solving or proposing to be able to solve.

This accomplishes a couple of things. One, it demonstrates that you understand current market pressures and the macro trends that drive them. Second, it forces you to train a spotlight on what you're aiming to tackle by ensuring it's an actual problem in the world.

If you're trying to franchise a chain of "freeze the fat" body-sculpting offices, you're not solving a problem. You're preying on human weakness for the purpose of turning one-dollar bills into two-dollar bills--with the yawning downside that almost anyone can do the same thing.

As an investment opportunity, your rich uncle Ned may jump all over this. But real investors want to solve real problems. If all you want is to turn a buck, skip the VC pitch meetings and buy vending machines.

Slide 4: Present your solution.

Your fourth slide should cover how you plan to solve the previously stated problem. It's a simple rundown of your value propositions, illustrating how you plan to address the crucial societal need you already identified faster, more effectively, and more affordably than ever before.

Surprisingly, infomercials tend to do a pretty fantastic job conveying this kind of information.

"For just three simple payments of just $9.99, it slices, dices, minces, purees--and cleanup is a breeze!" This slide will be a breeze too--if your solution is solid.

Slide 5: Answer "Why now?"

Investors are like mountain climbers looking for a foothold. Ideally, it comes in the form of a Eureka! moment that happens when a new technology overlays with a coinciding shift in societal needs.

The mass-market automobile. A streaming music services. The "Why now?" slide needs to focus on what's going on in your industry and society at large that makes the timing of your business so prescient.

This is where you get to stand on your soapbox and give a primer on all the things you know about the intricacies of your business, and how they match up with the dynamics of the market.

You should also touch on the competition: why nobody's doing this, how the people who are doing it aren't very good at it, and why you're uniquely poised to color in the resulting white space.

Feel free to be a great big, annoying know-it-all here. It's expected.

Slide 6: Explain how this will work.
This sounds pretty open-ended and hairy, but it's really just a short and simple explanation of your revenue model. Basically, how do you plan to make money? If you're running a digital content company, slide No. 6 might sound something like this:

"Our business works because we buy premium domain names, add unique content created by our world-class team, require consumers to register with their emails, and then sell their emails for $5 each to companies that want them--and we get paid up front."

Remember those Family Circus cartoons with the dotted trail that tracked the roaming shenanigans of little Jeffy? Slide 6 is pretty much that, but for the dollars that will be flowing into your business.

Slide 7: Spell out how your business will perform for the next five years.
Perhaps unsurprisingly, you're going to finish with two financial slides. This first one should map out the expected results of the business as told by the five narratives that matter: units sold, revenue, cost, yield, and customer acquisition cost over time. Obviously, there's an art to presenting all of this information in a way that shows your business as the most compelling money-spawning creation in recent history.
Prepare a simple line chart for the above information and know that slide No. 7 is a mere steppingstone to something much

more critical ...

Slide: 8: Show your investors how they'll 10x.
You've covered the problem, walked through your solution, your team, your timing, your revenue model--now it's time for the dramatic climax: how your potential investors can make a 10x return.

There's nothing rational about this particular number. It's just what humans who invest for a living have decided feels good. And it is all any investor will really care about--from a tiny, early-stage VC to a late-round institutional partner looking to fund you for the long term.

So, explain how it's going to happen for them--and don't be shy. Describe the cavernously huge addressable market you're tapping into. Demonstrate how you and your team plan to mine it to its core like a gang of crack roustabouts. And spell out how this will bring all involved the most insanely profitable investment of their careers.

If you can pull off all of the above in just eight slides, the folks across the table will doubt you at their peril, thank you for your brevity--and hopefully back you with their pocketbooks.

Wait...There is more!
To be clear, there are various other steps you can take to help tell your company's story in a more concise and tantalizing way to attract the attention and dollars of any prospective investors.

I am by no means suggesting that you simply prepare a Pitch deck and Elevator pitch, and that's it.

Once you start to line up some investor meetings, you will want to prepare any other documents that will show investors why they should take a chance on you and your company.

You will also want to enlist the help of a handful of professionals to help you get ready to present your company to VC's and Angel investors.

In the next chapter, I will delve a bit more into this topic.

You will want to prepare a detailed accounting of all your company's financials (if available), showing all income, revenue and profit numbers over any period of time.

You will also want to elicit endorsements from well-known vendors, partners and any letters of intent you may have from any potential buyers.

For Example, if you have a letter of intent from Target Corp. Proposing to sell your product in their 1,844 stores, you will want to communicate that with any potential investor, thereby demonstrating the future earning potential of your firm.

CHAPTER EIGHT

TEAM OF PROS

Don't aim for success if you want it; just do what you love and believe in, and it will come naturally.

– David Frost

Hire experts whenever you can. This is an opinion I have come to strongly hold after many years in business. Years filled with avoidable blunders, false starts, and dire consequences.

In business, and generally in life, really, it is important to seek the counsel of those who have deeper experience and knowledge than yourself.

To some inexperienced few, this may seem like a radical idea, a foreign concept even.

There are many reasons folks don't seek out the help of professionals when the occasion calls for it.

The two most common reasons are the **lack of funds** and the general feeling that "**We can it ourselves**".

Now, I will be the first to concede that in some situations, especially when starting a new business, we are better served by DIY-ing things till we can afford better.

In some instances, yes, you are better off spending the time to complete the task that requires completing, rather than spending money you don't have to hire a professional. I get it. Been there, done that.

When it comes to approaching investors, however, especially professional investors, you should try to build a team of professionals to help. There are many folks out there whose job it is to help entrepreneurs just like you find quality, qualified investors to help fund their businesses.

These types of professionals - if you find the right ones, will, or should have years of experience under their belt, and a whole host of contacts; and resources to help you position yourself to attract the funding you need.

You want to build a small team of professionals. Your "squad" should, at the very least consist of a qualified **Attorney**, one who has successfully helped other business folks find funding, an **Accountant** to help you prepare your financial records in a way that provides a full picture of your company's financial records, and a **Designated fundraiser**.

You will also want to partner with other members of the Investor class.

You can contact a local Angel Investor to see if they will be willing to take you under their wing. This person's main role will be to introduce you to other accredited investors, since, you know; Birds of a feather, and all that.

If you do nothing else, you should consult with the pros listed in this chapter.

Designated fundraiser
Let me first say that the Designated fundraiser does not have to be a pro. In fact, it is better if they are

not. This should be a member of your founding team whose only job during your capital raising efforts will be to interact with your multiple prospective backers (if applicable).

If you find yourself dealing with multiple parties who are looking at the option of investing in your company, choose one person to handle fundraising so the rest of your team can focus on running the business. Your Designated Fundraiser should, according to Paul Graham, renowned entrepreneur and venture capitalist, do their best to insulate the rest of your team from the details of the process.

According to the experts, the person who handles all fundraising activities should be the most formidable of all, preferably the Chief Executive. Outside of the normal procedural meetings that typically take place in these cases, Graham also suggests bringing the entire founding team to meet any potential investors who are looking to invest a significant amount and needs a meeting as a final step in their decision-making process.

Be sure not to take your eye off the ball in terms of the day-to-day operations at your company. Fundraising can be very time-consuming. Try not to let it slow down growth (too much) in your company.

Attorneys

Attorneys can play various vital roles when it comes to your fundraising campaign. How involved your lawyer is will depend on which method(s) you decide to use when soliciting capital for your business idea or startup company.

I generally prefer to enlist the help of a qualified Lawyer whenever I embark on any business, legal, or regulatory journey. I always feel better about any deal when, outside of my management team, I have a qualified attorney guiding my decisions every step of the way.

I strongly suggest seeking the help of an attorney with ample experience in helping startups raise capital.

A qualified Lawyers can help:

- Select an intermediary that meets your business's needs, as well as ensure that you meet the criteria to be listed on their website. If you choose to list shares in your company on some of the platforms I spoke about earlier, an attorney can help you complete the steps required to be featured on these sites.

- Make sure that you meet all financial disclosure requirements before your campaign begins.

- Ensure that you successfully complete your registration with the SEC and any other regulatory bodies (if applicable)

- Protect your business should you encounter a dispute, litigation, or action from an investor down the line.

- Introduce you to other entrepreneurs who have completed a successful campaign in the past so you can share ideas and gain insights. If your Lawyers knows no other entrepreneurs who have raised funds, that is a red flag.

These are but a few of the many important roles an attorney can play. It is my belief that in business, one should look at their relationship with general counsel as an ongoing one.

Think of your main attorney as the friend you call to make sure that you are on the right side of the law, and that you take steps to protect your interest whenever you have a great new idea.

They are there to help make sure that you color within the lines at all times. Your General Counsel can also be the guy or gal whose job it is to point you in the direction of other professionals and even other attorneys when the task at hand exceeds their area of expertise.

If your lawyer is competent/ talented and has your trust and confidence, then anyone they recommend will be folks of similar qualities.

Accountants
The role of an accountant when it comes to

fundraising for your startup begins long before you actually start talking to any potential Angels and/ or Venture firms.

As an entrepreneur, I would say that it is never too early to bring on an experienced accountant to help keep your records in order.

I know this may seem like an unnecessary step, especially while you are in the middle of launching your startup, or while you are in the eye of the storm trying to get your very first sales/customers. I mean, who has time for that, right? You should! Trust me, you will be glad (down the line) that you did.

You should maintain accurate records of all your financial transactions. Besides helping you stay on the good side of the Tax man, your Accountant should be consulted on your desire to, at some point solicit outside capital for your company.

He or she will help you prepare all the necessary financial documents and presentations needed to attract investors.

That being said, it helps to make sure that you, at the outset, retain the services of not just an experienced Accountant, but one who has worked with startups under similar circumstances. By that I mean, they have some experience working with companies that have been able to successfully raise funds.

As boring and unsexy as it may seem, your "financials" is the most compelling part of your pitch. This is not something the financial media outlets communicate very well.

Ever heard the saying "**If you ain't making no dollars, you ain't making no sense**"? This is true of startup businesses. Other than in cases where you are merely pitching a business **idea**, the most attractive business to professional investors is one that is profitable and growing fast. If you have these two things going for you, you will have no problem raising capital or getting banks to provide you with the funding you need.

The question at that point then becomes: which Investor(s) do you see yourself working with long-term? Keeping an eye on your company's financials is the best way to work towards profitability, even before you approach investors.

Fundraising Consultants
Firms like Campbell & Company are well positioned to help startup entrepreneurs such as yourself prepare to raise funds. These types of companies: Fundraising Consultants, serve as a one stop shop for all your fundraising needs. They typically charge a success fee and take shares in your company once they have successfully helped you attract and closed on new investor deals.

Among other functions, these types of consultants are able to:

- Help you evaluate your needs.
- Uncover your strengths and weaknesses.
- Assess your fundraising potential.
- Outline a plan of action (if you're ready).
- Help prepare materials for use in your

interactions with potential Inventors.

- Conduct training for you and your team.
- Troubleshoot any problems that come up during the entire process. And, serve as a catalyst to keep your campaign moving.

"None of us is as smart as all of us." --Ken Blanchard

No matter the case, always - in business and in life, try to bring as many like-minded people as you can in the pursuit of a great idea.

Teams accomplish great things! I often find this sentiment being overlooked by many entrepreneurs who tirelessly work to accomplish things on their own, often thinking that the only glory or success worth celebrating is one that is accomplished alone. The " **I did it all by myself**" factor. This type of thinking often precipitates inevitable failure.

Build a team around you. Create a big tent and fill it with true believers. I know that sounds really cult-like, but I promise you that if you seek to build things using the help of others who believe in you and what you are trying to do, you will be successful more times than not.

CHAPTER NINE

AVENUES

"I did then what I knew how to

do. Now that I know better, I do better."
— Maya Angelou

The purpose of this chapter is to provide you with specific suggestions and resources as it relates to some of the portals, platforms, and companies we have talked about in this book.

I will also provide you with information on other resources that I feel can be useful to you as you consider the option to solicit outside investors for your company or business idea.

Below are some resources that can help you along the way.

Venture Capital firms
The following are Venture Capital firms that are open to working with small businesses.

These firms are able to invest in deals that are smaller than the average VC deal.

5AM Ventures, Menlo Park, Calif.

5AM Ventures is a leading venture capital firm focused on building next-generation life science companies capable of delivering outstanding returns to our investors.

(http://5amventures.com/)

Early-stage investments (in millions, USD): $158

Industry: Pharmaceuticals and biotechnology

Assets under management (in millions, USD): $685

MPM Capital, Boston

MPM Capital is a healthcare investment firm with over two decades of experience founding and investing in life-sciences companies that seek to translate scientific innovations into cures for major diseases.

(http://www.mpmcapital.com/)

Early-stage investments (in millions, USD): $147

Industries: Healthcare devices and supplies, pharmaceuticals and biotechnology

Assets under management (in millions, USD): $2,113

Smartinvest Ventures, Wilmington, DE

SmartInvest is an early stage accelerator lead venture fund which has accelerated the growth of startups through their global reach and investments.

(https://www.smartinvestventures.com/)

Catapult Ventures, Los Altos, CA

They invest in companies at the intersection of hardware, embedded systems, and software. Leveraging the synergies between these domains can enable innovations that otherwise would not be possible. We look for founders who create a competitive advantage with interdisciplinary thinking.

(http://catapultventures.vc/)

Fundraising news
Below are a few websites and platforms that exist to provide entrepreneurs like yourself with the latest headlines, updates, tips, and insights on the ins and outs of the Venture capital world, as well as the latest deals, investor pitch conferences, interviews, and more.

TechCrunch

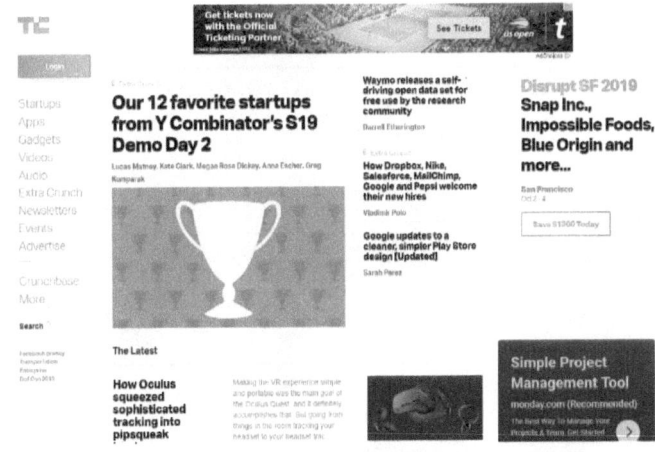

TechCrunch is an online magazine reporting on technology opinions, news, and analysis.

(https://techcrunch.com)

Crunchbase

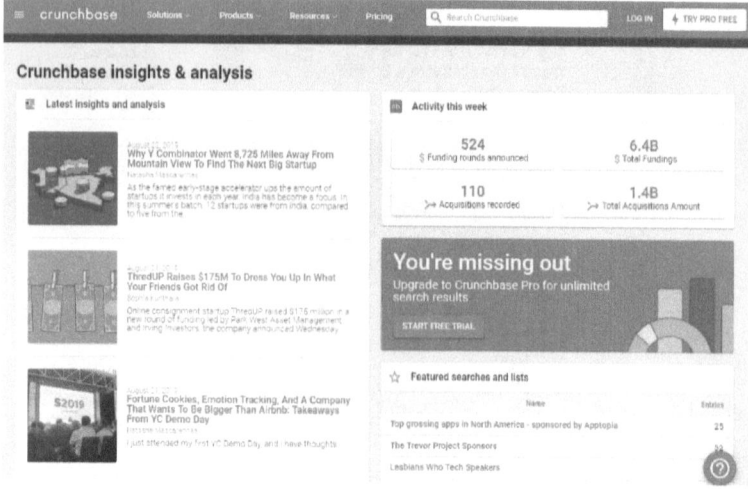

Crunchbase provides the latest insights and analysis of the VC and investing world as a whole. The portal provides details on the latest deals and companies looking for funding.

(https://www.crunchbase.com/)

Vator

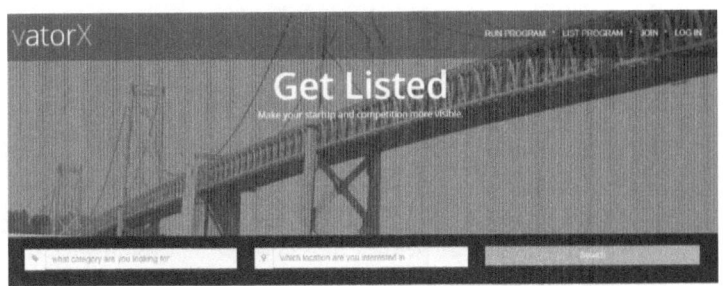

As one of the first online networks dedicated to startups and investors, Vator has brought to you in-depth interviews with some of today's most celebrated entrepreneurs, before they became household names.

(https://vator.tv/)

Startup incubators

A Startup Incubator is an organization that helps new and startup companies to develop by providing services such as management training or office space. The National Business Incubation Association (NBIA) defines business incubators as a catalyst tool for either regional or national economic development.

Entrepreneurs Roundtable Accelerator

(https://www.eranyc.com/)

ERA's four-month accelerator program consists of seed funding opportunities, hands-on help and collaboration with other startups in the program. The New York City-based company specializes in early-stage tech-based startups. Accepted startups receive an initial $40,000 investment and then spend the program in ERA's co-working space in Chelsea.

Launchpad LA

(http://launchpad.la/)

Launchpad LA offers accepted startups in its Southern California-based program between $25,000 and $100,000 along with free office space and access to mentors and advisors. To qualify, startups should be tech-based and either from, or able to relocate to the Los Angeles area.

StartFast

(http://startfast.net/)

This accelerator invites startups from around the world to apply for its three-month program. Accepted companies can earn up to $18,000 in funding as well as support from StartFast's entrepreneurial community and access to mentors and talent.

Angel Investor networks

An Angel investor is an affluent individual who provides capital for a business start-up, usually in exchange for convertible debt or ownership equity. Angel investors usually give support to start-ups at the initial moments and when most investors are not prepared to back them.

There are various Angel Investor groups out there that you can contact to help you get started on your fundraising campaign.

Being able to have an Angel in your corner, especially at the outset of your fundraising efforts will not just help you secure your first investor, but as I have said before, this will put you in a position to get warm introductions to other Angel Investors.

Below are a few Angel Networks. You can start with these as well as conduct your own research to find others that meet your needs.

Ohio TechAngel Funds, Columbus, Ohio
(http://www.ohiotechangels.com/)
Number of angels: 282

Who it helps: Supports early-stage Ohio-based information technology, advanced materials, and medical technology companies.

Tech Coast Angels, Los Angeles

(http://www.techcoastangels.com/)

Number of angels: 263

Who it helps: Provides connections, knowledge, mentoring and operational assistance to early-stage entrepreneurs in the tech, biotech, consumer products, Internet, information technology, life sciences, media, software and environmental markets.

Investors' Circle, San Francisco

(http://www.investorscircle.net/)

Number of angels: 225

Who it helps: Uses private capital to promote businesses that address social and environmental issues. The group has invested almost $150 million in 225 companies, it says.

Golden Seeds LLC, New York City

(http://www.goldenseeds.com/)

Number of angels: 190

Who it helps: Members invest directly, or through a managed fund, in companies that are founded by or led by women. Sectors include consumer products, technology, software and life sciences.

Alliance of Angels, Seattle

(http://www.allianceofangels.com/)

Number of angels: 100

Who it helps: Early-stage investors in startups based in the Northwest region of the country.

Pasadena Angels, Altadena, Calif.

(http://www.pasadenaangels.com/)

Number of angels: 100

Who it helps: Provides up to $750,000 in early-stage and seed financing to startups in southern California.

Business Plan Software

Liveplan

LivePlan simplifies business planning, budgeting, forecasting, and performance tracking for small businesses and startups.

(https://www.liveplan.com)

Pitch Deck templates

What is a business pitch deck?

A business pitch deck is a presentation that provides an overview of your business plan to your audience.

Typically, you would present a pitch deck to potential investors, business partners, board members, and clients.

Below are a few platforms from which you can obtain and customize pitch decks to help with your fundraising.

Venngage

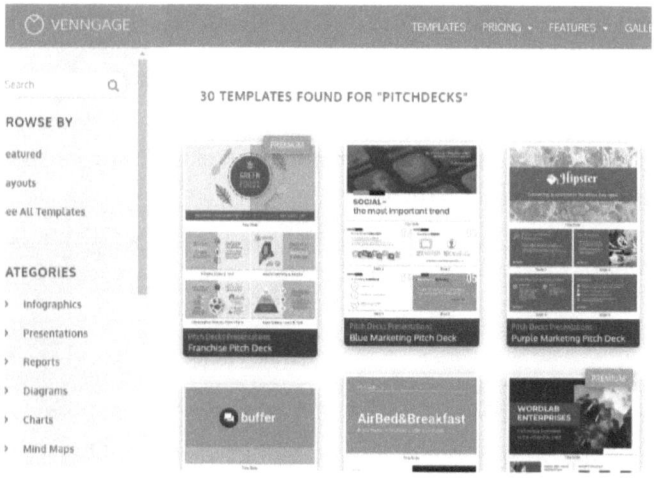

Access thousands of highly-customizable pitch decks

(https://venngage.com/templates/search/PITCHD ECKS)

Canva

A more popular option, Canva provides thousands of pitch decks ready to be customized and used for free.

(https://www.canva.com/templates/search/pitch-deck%20presentations/)

Equity Crowdfunding sites

Equity Crowdfunding sites allow entrepreneurs from all over the country to list their companies and allow investors to review and make investments in these firms.

Equity Crowdfunding has become very popular among entrepreneurs who are looking to raise significant sums of money to grow their businesses but don't have the appetite, or budgets to engage fully in the more traditional fundraising processes.

Equity Crowdfunding was made possible due to the passage of the **The Jumpstart Our Business Startups Act, or JOBS Act,** in 2012.

Crowdfunder

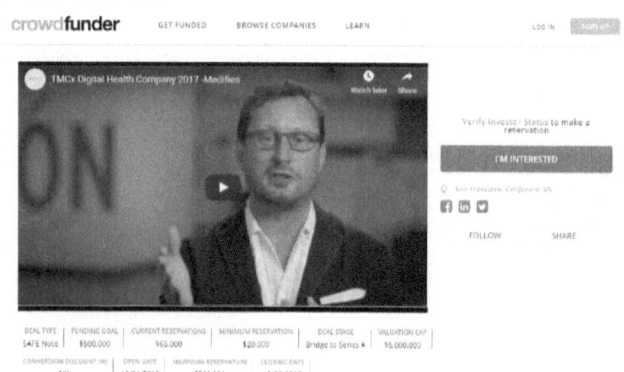

Crowdfunder was launched in Los Angeles in 2012 with a mission to, in the company's own words, "empower thousands of entrepreneurs to grow high-impact ventures." The company provides the following figures regarding equity funding services:

- $160,000,000 in investment commitments on the platform
- 12,000 individual & institutional investors
- 36,000 companies
- Funded 100+ deals with an average deal size of $1.8M

Fundable

Founded in 2012 and based in Ohio, Fundable is an

unusual crowdfunding site in it hosts host both rewards and equity crowdfunding campaigns. Think of it as both a Kickstarter-type platform and an equity crowdfunder. Given the subject of this article, however, I'll be focusing on the equity side.

SeedInvest

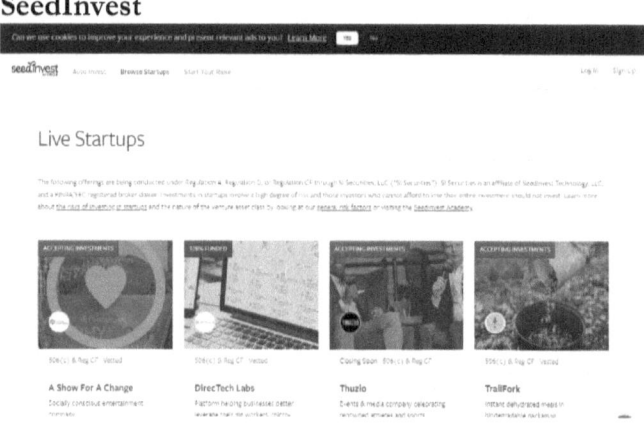

(https://www.seedinvest.com/)

SeedInvest was founded in 2012 just as the JOBS Act was being signed into law. In fact, founders Ryan Feit and James Han were part of the movement to get the Act passed in the first place. Like Wefunder, they offer Regulation Crowdfunding, opening up investing to the masses.

CHAPTER TEN

NUMBERS DON'T LIE

"If people like you, they'll listen to you, but if they trust you, they'll do business with you."
— Zig Ziglar

I wrote this book to help you think about and prepare to possibly talk to investors. I am assuming you either have an idea for a great business, or you have already started a business, exhausted all the cash you could get from your friends and family, and are now looking to talk to some "real investors".

Now, I can understand that even after reading this book you will have some more questions. Questions relating to the process of raising capital, and / or ways to return value to your initial investors and founders.

There was no way I was going to be able to cover all the pertinent fundraising topics in this book. For that, I apologize. I will, however, encourage you to seek out as much information as you can.

Information that will not only help you with your fundraising campaign, but also help you build a stronger, more profitable business.

In an effort to provide you with an overview of where we, the entrepreneurial, and investing community stand, I will provide you with some statistical data as it relates to the current state of startup investing and entrepreneur sentiment.

2019 STARTUP OUTLOOK US REPORT
Source: www.svb.com

Business Conditions

MANY US STARTUPS EXPECT BUSINESS

CONDITIONS TO IMPROVE

60% of entrepreneurs surveyed believed that business conditions will improve as compared to 2018. 9% think conditions will take a turn for the worse.

Describe your outlook on business conditions for your company this year compared with 2018.

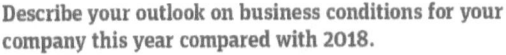

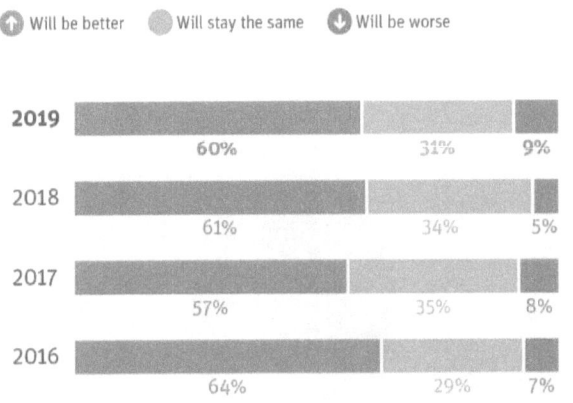

Funding

RAISING CAPITAL GROWS EASIER IN THE PAST TWO YEARS

Seventy-one percent of US startups surveyed successfully raised capital in 2018. Of those, one-quarter say the current fundraising environment is not challenging. VCs and private equity firms have been investing larger rounds in fewer deals, focusing their capital on high-performing startups; however, pre-revenue companies and those with smaller revenue streams describe raising capital as considerably more challenging.

What is your view of the current fundraising environment?

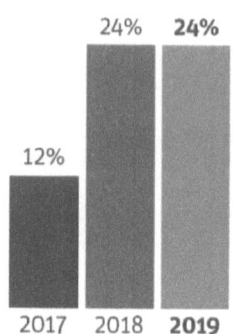

Not challenging

24% **24%**

12%

2017 2018 **2019**

Note: Asked of private companies that successfully raised capital.

VENTURE CAPITAL IS THE GO-TO SOURCE OF FUNDING

Alternative financing sources are a topic of great discussion among startups and the media. Still, half of US startups say they expect their next source of funding to be venture capital — a steady level over the past three years. Another 17 percent say they expect to tap small or individual investors for their next funding round.

What do you expect to be your company's next source of funding?

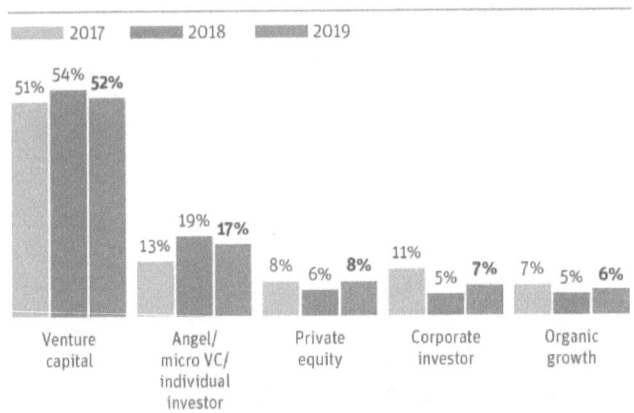

2017   2018   2019

	Venture capital	Angel/ micro VC/ individual investor	Private equity	Corporate investor	Organic growth
2017	51%	13%	8%	11%	7%
2018	54%	19%	6%	5%	5%
2019	52%	17%	8%	7%	6%

Note: Asked of private US companies that successfully raised capital. Other sources of funding include bank debt, IPOs, mergers, government grants, ICOs and crowd funding and represented 10% in 2017, 11% in 2018 and 10% in 2019.

STARTUPS SAY THE MOST REALISTIC GOAL IS ACQUISITION

Several unicorns are lining up for possible 2019 IPOs. But most US startups say their more realistic long-term goal is to be acquired — long cited as the most common path to an exit. A larger percentage of startups compared with a year ago say they don't know what their ultimate goal is, underscoring the difficulty of planning an exit amid increased market volatility.

What is the realistic long-term goal for your company?

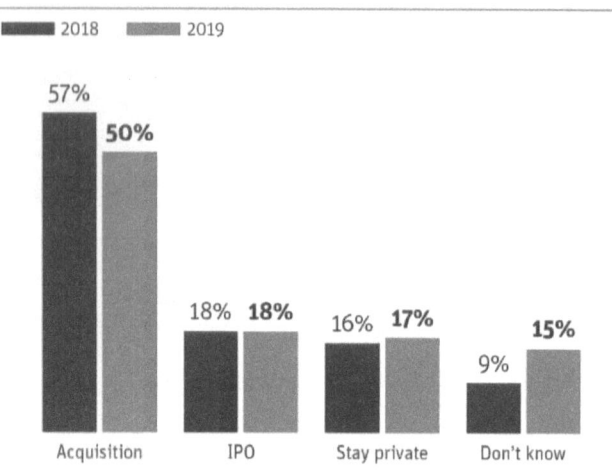

M&A ACTIVITY IS HEALTHY

Nearly 90 percent of US startups believe that M&A activity will maintain 2018 levels or increase. With plentiful capital available, many corporations, private equity funds and scaling companies have the resources to make acquisitions.

How do you think the M&A market will change in 2019?

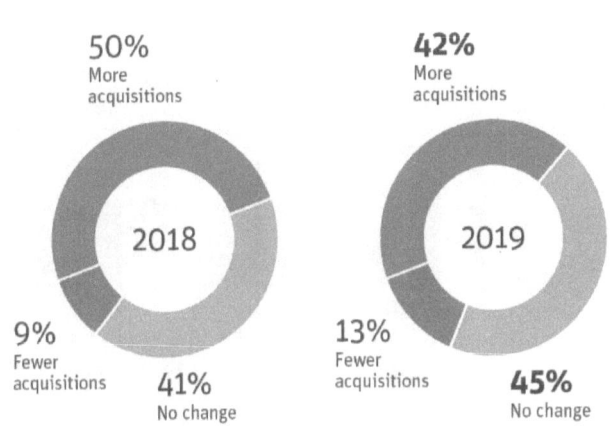

50%
More
acquisitions

42%
More
acquisitions

2018

2019

9%
Fewer
acquisitions

41%
No change

13%
Fewer
acquisitions

45%
No change

AI IS THE MOST PROMISING SECTOR NOW — AND IN THE FUTURE

US entrepreneurs say AI and big data are the technologies with the most promise today. Looking ahead a decade, they expect autonomous transportation to make the biggest leap in potential, taking the second spot after AI.

Which areas will be the most promising in the innovation economy?

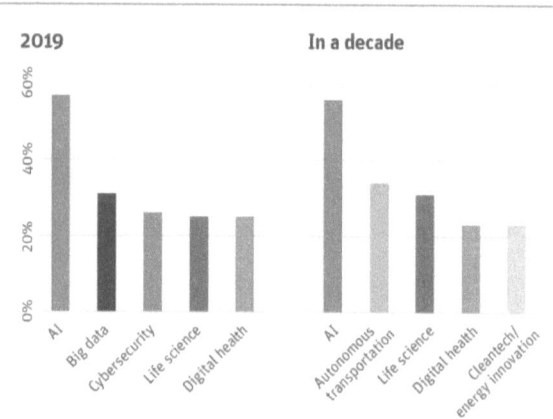

Note: Respondents could choose up to three responses.

Hiring & Talent

STARTUPS PLAN TO HIRE BUT FIND TALENT SEARCH HARD

More than 80 percent of US startups say they plan to add employees in 2019, but 29 percent recognize it is extremely challenging to find talent with the necessary skills to grow their businesses. Another 62 percent say it is somewhat challenging. Startups are most in need of filling product development/R&D, sales and technical positions.

What are your projections for hiring new employees in 2019?

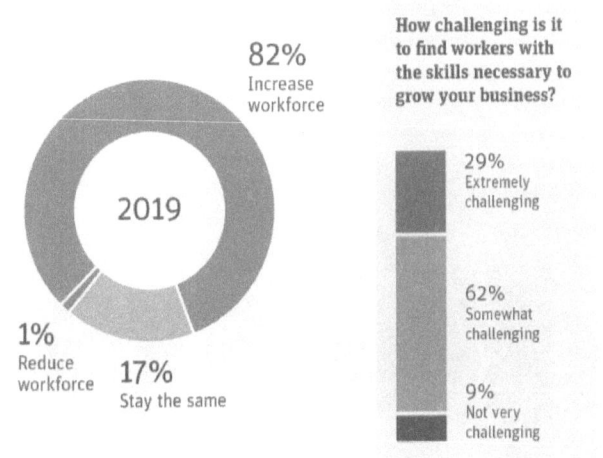

82%
Increase workforce

2019

1%
Reduce workforce

17%
Stay the same

How challenging is it to find workers with the skills necessary to grow your business?

29%
Extremely challenging

62%
Somewhat challenging

9%
Not very challenging

WOMEN ARE GAINING MORE STARTUP LEADERSHIP ROLES

The focus on gender parity in the innovation ecosystem has increased in recent years. While there is still work to be done, US startups are reporting some progress. The percentage of startups with at least one woman on the board of directors has increased to 37 percent — the highest level since SVB started tracking in 2015. The percentage of startups with at least one woman in an executive position is 53 percent, an increase of 10 percentage points compared with last year.

Percentage of startups with at least one woman in a leadership position:

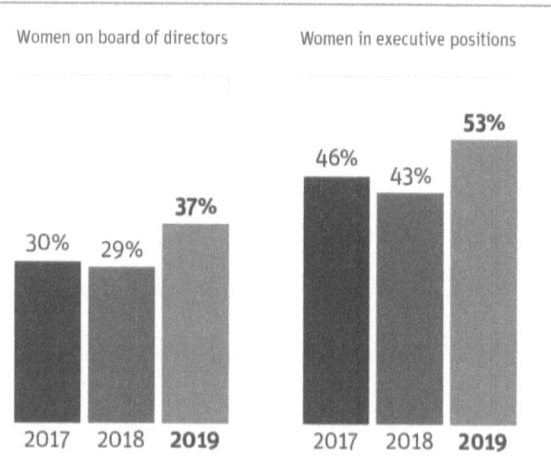

Women on board of directors

2017	2018	2019
30%	29%	**37%**

Women in executive positions

2017	2018	2019
46%	43%	**53%**

ACCESS TO TALENT IS THE TOP POLICY CONCERN

As in past years, a majority of US startups say access to talent is the most important public policy issue affecting companies like theirs. Concern over healthcare costs for employees and cybersecurity also rank highly. And more startups are citing consumer privacy than in the past.

What are the most important public policy issues affecting companies like yours?

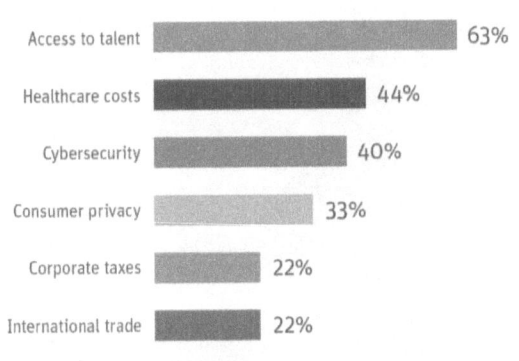

Access to talent	63%
Healthcare costs	44%
Cybersecurity	40%
Consumer privacy	33%
Corporate taxes	22%
International trade	22%

Note: Respondents could choose up to three responses.

MANY US STARTUPS ARE UNEASY ABOUT CHINA TRADE POLICY

Half of US startups say they are concerned that trade policy between the US and China will hurt their businesses in 2019. Two-thirds of Chinese startups express concern about a negative impact.

How concerned are you that trade policy between China and the US will negatively impact your business in 2019?

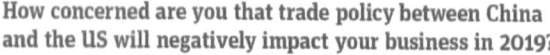

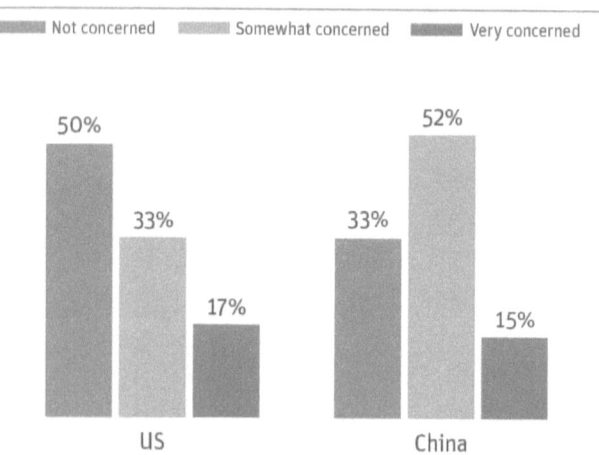

WHERE YOU STAND

Please note that the above is but a snippet taken from a larger overview of global investor trends and small business and entrepreneur sentiment.

I provided this information to help you get a fuller, more quantifiable understanding of where we stand as a global economy and what impact these trends can have on your business growth prospects and your desire to get out there and try to raise capital for your company.

Please note that, in the above, I only present small business sentiment and trends as told by U.S Investors and entrepreneurs.

For a more panoramic global view, please visit https://www.svb.com/startup-outlook-report-2019/us

CHAPTER ELEVEN

BUILD IT, AND THEY WILL COME

"Quality is more important than quantity. One home run is much better than two doubles."
– Steve Jobs

Much is made on TV, and elsewhere about the processes through which entrepreneurs raise investment capital to start or grow their businesses. There are over three or four primetime shows based on this topic, and that's not even counting all the magazines, blogs, and websites that focus on this particular topic.

Listening to the so-called experts, it is easy to

get swept up by the pageantry of it all. No one ever talks about the fundamentals of business anymore. You will never hear a VC / consultant stress the need to build stable businesses. One with great products, and a focus on great customer service and profitability.

Investors like businesses, not ideas.

There seems to be a general misconception out there among most entrepreneurs. And it goes like this: "*I have a business idea, I asked my friends and family who all agree that this is a great idea, so I will go out and find investors to invest in my idea*". Of course, this is not how it works, generally.

Investors make that "experienced investors", the ones who do it for a living do not invest in ideas. Sure, you will probably be able to get your rich uncle or retired Grandma to come along with you financially to explore the viability of a great idea. That could work.

For "real investors" though, this is a non-starter. What investors look for are great companies with the potential to grow. Companies that have real customers, a great product or service, a unique business advantage, and a plan to grow. These are the opportunities investors look for.

Hidden Angels

Besides contacting Angels, and/ or Angel Networks directly, you can also put yourself in front of those who might, for the first time invest in a startup. You can do so by networking with affluent folks in your community.

If you choose to go this route, I would recommend that you don't just try to rub shoulders with the "Rich" but try to make it to events that are not necessarily organized for entrepreneurs to pitch ideas.

Nope, these types of events will be filled with hungry folks just like you, and every wealthy guy or gal there will have their guard up.

Try to make it to events that are filled with retired folks. Not just any retired folks but folks who were in business for themselves or worked in some kind of upper management positions. These types of folks tend to go out and invest in businesses as something to keep them busy during retirement years.

They also typically retire after selling their companies or cashing their company stocks in. This means that these types of folks are typically sophisticated as it relates to the innerworkings of businesses and are flushed with cash.

My wife's uncle, for example decided to go out to rural Kenya to build a medical facility as a way to spend his retirement years. You want to be around folks like that.

Great products, awesome customers
Believe me when I tell you that your number one goal, that is if you are at the "ideas" stage of your business journey is it to have a great product on the market.

Great products and services do not sell themselves, yes, this is true, but they do keep customers and users coming back for more.

Great products transcend gimmicks and out-of-the-box marketing schemes. Sure, building a great product, if you are anything like me, will take some time. The Version #1 of most products I build are never the best version. Not even close. I will admit that, but the thing is, I keep working on making whatever product I am rolling out better.

Once you get to the apex of product supremacy, you will see most of your customers start to stay on longer. You will start to see repeat business. This is a very profitable place to be if you offer a subscription product or a service or product that customers will need to replenish frequently.

One of my Companies, Feetly (www.fettly.com) is a great example of this phenomenon. We sell nutritional products online. Most of our customers buy from us at least once a week. They are typically more than happy to rant and rave about how great our products are, and how fast our shipping is.

This brings in new customers. All this helps reduce our marketing cost as we ship out more products.

Value works

Don't get caught up in the hype and culture of fundraising. I know how strange this statement sounds coming from a guy who just wrote a whole book on the topic. What I mean is, do not get addicted to raising money just for the sake of it. And yes, that is an actual thing.

There are folks out there who seem to be in the business of raising capital as opposed to building their businesses. They spend more time attending fancy investor conferences and pitch events. They seem to enjoy sitting around talking about term sheets and valuations rather than seeing to the day-to-day operations at their firms. And can you blame them? As much attention as the media pays to which companies are worth what, and which is a Unicorn, it is easy for entrepreneurs to fall for the valuation race.

The dot com bubble was caused by this kind of behavior (Check out the movie startup.com).

I recommend spending most of your time building value. Value for your employees, partners, and customers. This is how you will be able to, when the time comes, deliver on the promise of ROI to your investors.

ABOUT THE AUTHOR

Frank is Co-Founder of Corvus Web Services, a full-service software services development firm.

He is also a serial entrepreneur with investments and interests in many industries including real estate, eCommerce, financial services, and publishing.

NOTES

https://www.svb.com/startup-outlook-report-2019/us

https://www.seedinvest.com/offerings

https://venngage.com/templates/search/PITCH DECKS

https://www.fundable.com/

https://www.crowdfunder.com/medifies2/invest

https://www.merchantmaverick.com/the-7-best-equity-crowdfunding-sites-for-businesses-and-entrepreneurs/

https://www.canva.com/templates/search/pitch-deck%20presentations/

https://www.liveplan.com/?pm=HALFOFFMONTH1&utm_source=google&utm_medium=cpc&utm_campaign=liveplan_shopping&gclid=EAIaIQobChMIzNDkleCW5AIVho7ICh3TpgR2EAYYASABEgKug_D_BwE

https://www.entrepreneur.com/article/220149

https://www.eranyc.com/

https://smallbiztrends.com/2013/11/list-of-startup-incubators.html

https://vator.tv/x

https://www.crunchbase.com/

https://techcrunch.com/startups/

https://pitchbook.com/news/venture-capital

http://catapultventures.vc/news/

https://www.flightwave.aero/

http://www.mpmcapital.com/

http://5amventures.com/

https://www.entrepreneur.com/article/242702

https://medium.com/swlh/startup-accelerators-the-industry-and-its-current-state-in-2018-e40dd61ceb39

https://averillsolutions.com/fundraising-consultant-fees/

https://www.toptal.com/finance/startup-funding-consultants/fundraising-consultants-broker-dealers

https://www.khanacademy.org/economics-finance-domain/core-finance/stock-and-bonds/venture-capital-and-capital-markets/v/an-ipo

https://www.inc.com/scott-painter/want-to-raise-venture-capital-these-are-only-8-slides-your-pitch-deck-needs.html

https://www.mindtools.com/pages/article/elevator-pitch.htm

https://shockwaveinnovations.com/answering-the-exit-strategy-question/

https://www.thebalancesmb.com/funny-change-quotes-2892521

https://www.allbusiness.com/7-things-fix-business-approaching-vc-17314-1.html/2

HOW TO PREPARE YOUR
COMPANY OR BUSINESS IDEA
FOR OUTSIDE INVESTORS

FRANK DAPPAH

Co-Founder of Corvus
Web Services

HOW TO PREPARE YOUR
COMPANY OR BUSINESS IDEA
FOR OUTSIDE INVESTORS

PIXIE
DUST

FRANK DAPPAH

Co-Founder of Corvus
Web Services